Speaking Palauan:

SHAPES & COLORS
Bekbedengel

Palauan - English

Kalista Marbou

Illustrated by Lubei Cavin

This book belongs to:

Copyright 2020 Morets Publishing
Shapes & Colors
"Bekbedengel"

All rights reserved. No part of this book
may be reproduced in any manner whatsoever
without written permission in writing from the publisher.

Thank you for buying an authorized edition of
this book and for complying with copyright laws by
not reproducing, scanning or distributing
any part of it in any form
without permission.

For information visit SpeakingPalauan.com
Written by Kalista Marbou
Illustrations by Lubei Cavin
ISBN: 9781736227237 (paperback)
ISBN 9781736227244 (ebook)

Printed in the United States of America
10 9 8 7 6 5 4 3 2 1
First Edition January 2021

Speaking Palauan Books are a series of books by Morets Publishing. These books are developed for local Palauan children, and those raised abroad to use as reading materials and learning tools of the language.

Bekbedengel is a book of shapes and colors presented in the vernacular. It is an aid to help children acquire the language of their mother tongue, and also to help them increase their use of speaking in Palauan. Parents are encouraged to read with their children and to help them pronounce each word. Our goal is for children to develop bilingual proficiency in reading, writing and speaking skills.

Copyright 2020 Morets Publishing
Shapes & Colors
"Bekbedengel"

All rights reserved. No part of this book
may be reproduced in any manner whatsoever
without written permission in writing from the publisher.

Thank you for buying an authorized edition of
this book and for complying with copyright laws by
not reproducing, scanning or distributing
any part of it in any form
without permission.

For information visit SpeakingPalauan.com
Written by Kalista Marbou
Illustrations by Lubei Cavin
ISBN: 9781736227237 (paperback)
ISBN 9781736227244 (ebook)

Printed in the United States of America
10 9 8 7 6 5 4 3 2 1
First Edition January 2021

Speaking Palauan Books are a series of books by Morets Publishing. These books are developed for local Palauan children, and those raised abroad to use as reading materials and learning tools of the language.

Bekbedengel is a book of shapes and colors presented in the vernacular. It is an aid to help children acquire the language of their mother tongue, and also to help them increase their use of speaking in Palauan. Parents are encouraged to read with their children and to help them pronounce each word. Our goal is for children to develop bilingual proficiency in reading, writing and speaking skills.

Blebelel

Ngklel a bleob / kata el ngar er ngii er a tekoi er a Belau

Shapes

Names of shapes in Palauan

Kliuar / Skak

Square

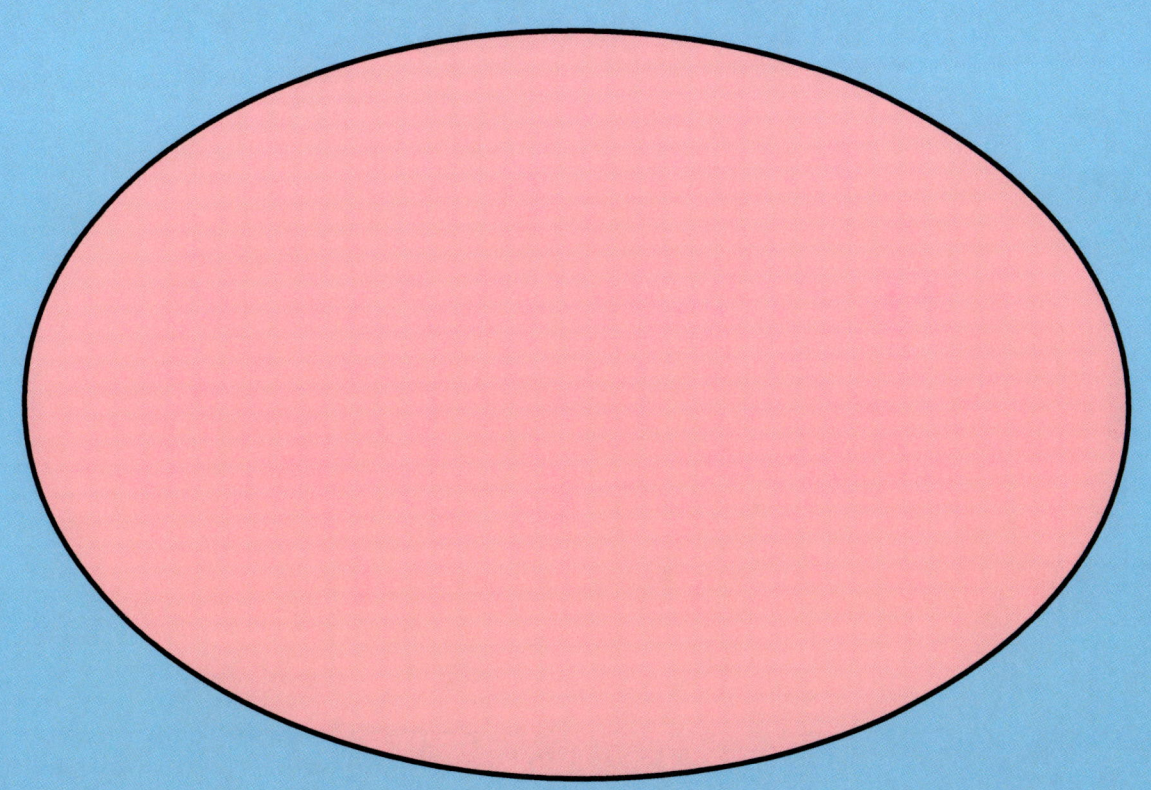

Derabahol

Rectangle

Delsemiich

Diamond

Sausab

Heart

Bedengel

Ngklel a bedengel / chiro el ngar er ngii er a tekoi er a Belau

Colors
Names of colors in Palauan

Becheleleu
White

Bedengel a Chudel

Green

Bedengel a Chutem

Brown

Bekerekard

Red

Bibrurek / Mellil

Yellow

Chedelekelek

Black

Cheriich

Reddish Brown

Mellemau

Blue

Kuk di bebil er a ngklel a chiro — Other color names

Bechachas	●	Black
Becheliliol	○	Very white
Bebibrurek	●	Yellowish
Bekekerekard	●	Reddish
Cheririich	●	Light Reddish Brown
Melellemau	●	Light Blue / Bluish

Ileakl a usbechel el chiro — Certain colors

Chetitau	●	Brown (skin)
Tatirou (el ua usaker)	●	Red cloth (loincloth)
Ulalk	●	Purple color or dye (pandanus dyed purple)

Made in the USA
Las Vegas, NV
18 July 2024